Easy Fudge Cookbook

A Fudge Cookbook for Fudge Lovers, Filled with Delicious Fudge Recipes

By
BookSumo Press
All rights reserved

Published by
http://www.booksumo.com

ENJOY THE RECIPES?

KEEP ON COOKING
WITH 6 MORE FREE COOKBOOKS!

Visit our website and simply enter your email address to join the club and receive your 6 cookbooks.

- http://booksumo.com/magnet
- https://www.instagram.com/booksumopress/
- https://www.facebook.com/booksumo/

LEGAL NOTES

All Rights Reserved. No Part Of This Book May Be Reproduced Or Transmitted In Any Form Or By Any Means. Photocopying, Posting Online, And / Or Digital Copying Is Strictly Prohibited Unless Written Permission Is Granted By The Book's Publishing Company. Limited Use Of The Book's Text Is Permitted For Use In Reviews Written For The Public.

Table of Contents

Fudge Filled Circles 7

Fudge Chubbies 8

Smooth Fudge Topping 9

Fudge Squares 10

No-Bake Fudge Bark 11

How to Make Fudge Glaze 12

Spicy Mexican Vegan Fudge Truffles 13

Authentic Dublin Fudge 14

Country Fudge Pie 15

Semisweet Valentine's Cookies 16

Country Fudge 17

Zesty Fudge 18

Fudge Kisses 19

Parisian Nutty Fudge 20

Oven Fudge 21

Berry Fudge 22

Buttery Peanut Fudge 23

August's Cheesecake 24

Fiesta Berry Brownies 25

Nutty Fudge for November 27

Food Cake Cookies 28

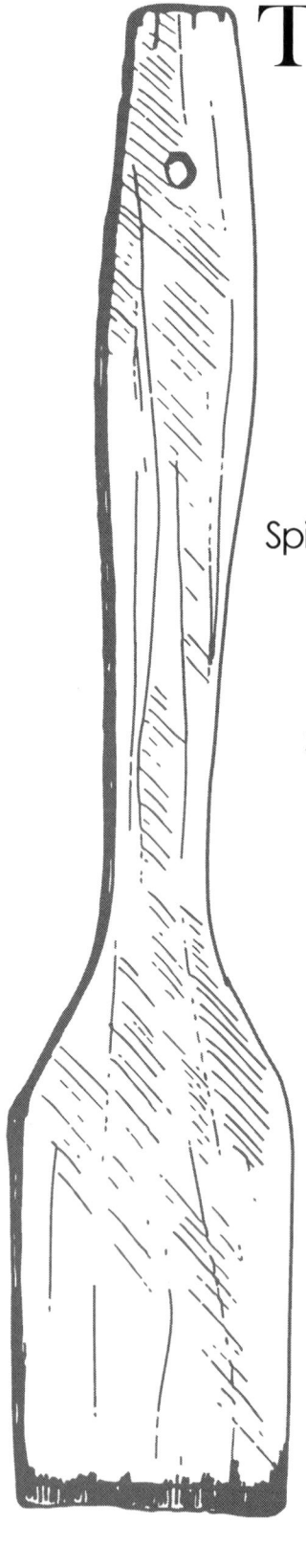

Fudge Oat Rectangles 29
Candy Gravy 30
Caribbean Creamy Fudge 31
3-Ingredient Peanut Butter Candy 32
Lover's Fudge Sauce 33
Waldorf Fudge 34
Gloria's Fudge Dip 35
Pecan Snack 36
Swiss Candy Fudge 37
Fudge on a Stick 38
Fudge in Moscow 39
November Only Fudge 40
Microwave Chocolate Butter 41
Cream Cheese Fudge 42
Morning Coffee Fudge 43
Fudge Mud Drink 44
Fudge Lunch Box Crisps 45
Fudge Milk 46
Christmas Fudge Drink 47
Maria's Cinnamon Fudge 48
5-Ingredient Pralines 49
Canadian Style Fudge 50

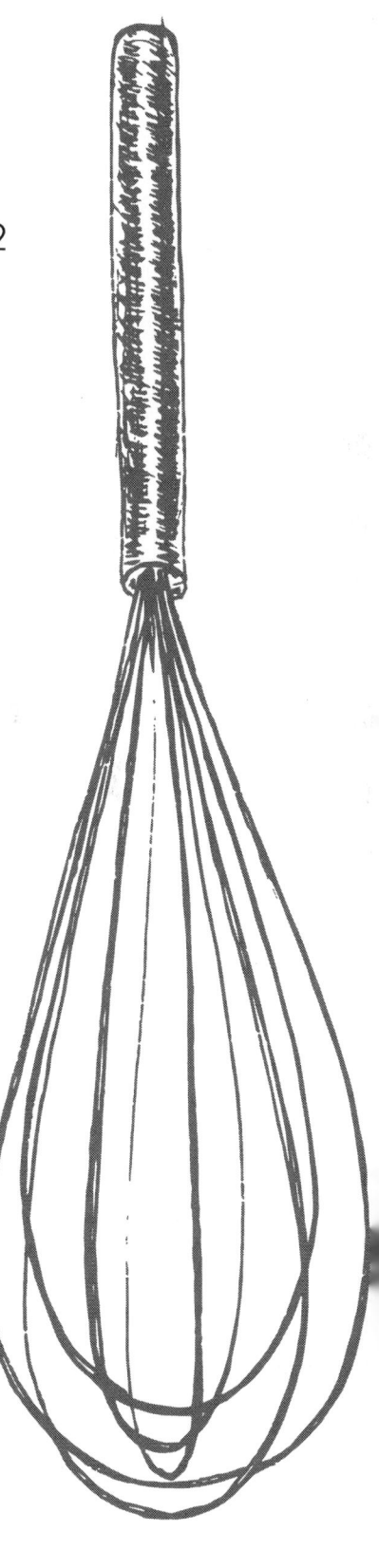

4-Ingredient Fudge Shells 51

Fudge Festivals 52

Fudge Spheres 53

Purple Flower Fudge 54

Fudge Tarts 55

Yellow Parfait 56

Fudge Filled Circles

Prep Time: 15 mins
Total Time: 45 mins

Servings per Recipe: 24
Calories   273 kcal
Fat   14.7 g
Carbohydrates   33.2g
Protein   4.9 g
Cholesterol   25 mg
Sodium   165 mg

Ingredients

- 1/2 C. butter, softened
- 1/2 C. creamy peanut butter
- 1/2 C. white sugar
- 1/2 C. packed brown sugar
- 1 egg
- 1/2 tsp vanilla extract
- 1 1/4 C. all-purpose flour
- 3/4 tsp baking soda
- 1/2 tsp salt
- 1 C. milk chocolate chips
- 1 C. semi-sweet chocolate chips
- 1 14 oz. can sweetened condensed milk
- 1 tsp vanilla extract
- 3/4 C. pecan halves

Directions

1. Set your oven to 325 degrees F before doing anything else and lightly, grease two 24 cups mini muffin tins.
2. In a large bowl, sift together the flour, baking soda and salt. In another bowl, add the butter, peanut butter and both sugars and beat till creamy.
3. Add the egg and 1/2 tsp of the vanilla and beat till well combined. Add the flour mixture into butter mixture and mix till a dough forms. Make about 1-inch sized 48 balls from the dough.
4. Place the ball into prepared muffin tins. Cook in the oven for about 14-16 minutes.
5. Meanwhile for filling, in a double boiler, place the chocolate chips on simmering water.
6. Add the milk and vanilla and mix well.
7. Remove the muffin tins from the oven and immediately with a melon baller, make a well in the center of each ball.
8. Keep the muffin tins onto wire rack to cool in the pan for about 5 minutes.
9. Then carefully, invert onto wire racks.
10. Fill each shell with the chocolate mixture evenly and serve with a topping of a pecan half.

FUDGE
Chubbies

🥣 Prep Time: 15 mins
🕐 Total Time: 1 hr 30 mins

Servings per Recipe: 16
Calories   130 kcal
Fat   8.3 g
Carbohydrates   14.7g
Protein   1.6 g
Cholesterol   21 mg
Sodium   22 mg

Ingredients

1/2 C. semisweet chocolate chips
5 tbsp unsalted butter
1 egg
1 tsp vanilla extract
1/3 C. white sugar
1/4 C. all-purpose flour
1/2 tsp baking powder

2 tbsp unsweetened cocoa powder, preferably Dutch-process
1 pinch salt
1/3 C. chopped walnuts
1/3 C. semisweet chocolate chips
1/3 C. raisins

Directions

1. In a microwave-safe bowl, add 1/2 C. of the chocolate chips and butter and microwave on High for about 1 minute.
2. Stir well and microwave till melted completely, stirring after every 20 seconds.
3. Remove from the microwave and keep aside to cool slightly.
4. In another bowl, add the egg, vanilla and sugar and beat till a thick and pale mixture forms.
5. Add the chocolate mixture and stir to combine.
6. In a third bowl, mix together the flour, baking powder, cocoa powder and salt.
7. Add the flour mixture into the chocolate mixture and mix till just combined.
8. Fold in the walnuts, remaining chocolate chips and raisins and refrigerate, covered for about 1 hour.
9. Set your oven to 325 degrees F and line a baking sheet with the parchment paper.
10. Make balls with the heaping tbspfuls of the dough and arrange onto the prepared baking sheets about 2-inch apart.
11. With your fingers, flatten each ball slightly. Cook in the oven for about 13-15 minutes.
12. Remove from the oven and keep the baking sheet on a cooling rack to cool.

Smooth Fudge Topping

Prep Time: 5 mins
Total Time: 15 mins

Servings per Recipe: 8
Calories	161 kcal
Fat	4.9 g
Carbohydrates	28.8g
Protein	2 g
Cholesterol	14 mg
Sodium	191 mg

Ingredients

- 1 C. white sugar
- 3 tbsp unsweetened cocoa powder
- 1/2 tsp salt
- 1 tsp ground cinnamon
- 3/4 C. evaporated milk
- 1 tsp vanilla extract
- 2 tbsp butter

Directions

1. In a medium pan, mix together the sugar, cocoa, salt and cinnamon.
2. Add the evaporated milk and bring to a boil on medium-high heat, stirring continuously.
3. Cook for 2 minutes, stirring continuously.
4. Remove from the heat and stir in the vanilla and butter.

FUDGE
Squares

🥣 Prep Time: 15 mins
🕐 Total Time: 45 mins

Servings per Recipe: 30
Calories   296 kcal
Fat   13.5 g
Carbohydrates   42g
Protein   4.2 g
Cholesterol   31 mg
Sodium   296 mg

Ingredients

2 C. light brown sugar
3/4 C. butter, softened
2 eggs
2 tsp vanilla extract
2 1/2 C. baking mix
3 C. quick cooking oats
2 C. semisweet chocolate chips

1 14 oz. can sweetened condensed milk
2 tbsp butter
1/2 tsp salt
1 C. chopped pecans
2 tbsp vanilla extract

Directions

1. Set your oven to 375 degrees F before doing anything else and lightly, grease a 13x9-inch baking dish.
2. In a large bowl, add the brown sugar, 3/4 C. of the butter, eggs and 2 tsp of the vanilla and mix till well combined.
3. Add the baking mix and oats and mix well and keep aside.
4. For the filling in a pan, add the chocolate chips, condensed milk, 2 tbsp of the butter and salt on low heat.
5. Cook, stirring continuously till smooth.
6. Remove from the heat and stir in the pecans and 2 tbsp of the vanilla.
7. Place about 2/3 of the oatmeal mixture in the bottom of the prepared baking dish and with the back of spoon, press to smooth the top surface.
8. Place chocolate mixture over the oatmeal mixture evenly and top with the remaining oatmeal mixture.
9. Cook in the oven for about 30 minutes.
10. Refrigerate to cool completely before serving.

No-Bake Fudge Bark

Prep Time: 5 mins
Total Time: 10 mins

Servings per Recipe: 48
Calories	186 kcal
Fat	8.5 g
Carbohydrates	27.7 g
Protein	1.8 g
Cholesterol	11 mg
Sodium	38 mg

Ingredients

- 2 C. white sugar
- 2 C. packed brown sugar
- 1 C. butter
- 1 C. milk
- 2 C. semisweet chocolate chips
- 4 C. quick cooking oats
- 1 C. chopped walnuts
- 1 C. flaked coconut

Directions

1. In a large bowl, mix together the oats, nuts, coconut and chocolate chips.
2. In a pan, add the sugars, butter and milk and bring to a boil.
3. Boil for about 2 minutes.
4. Place the hot butter mixture over the oat mixture and mix well.
5. With a tsp, place the mixture onto a wax paper lined cookie sheet in a single layer.
6. Refrigerate to set completely.

HOW TO MAKE
Fudge Glaze

🥣 Prep Time: 15 mins
🕐 Total Time: 30 mins

Servings per Recipe: 16
Calories   84 kcal
Fat   4.3 g
Carbohydrates   12g
Protein   0.6 g
Cholesterol   8 mg
Sodium   25 mg

Ingredients

1 1/2 1 oz. squares unsweetened chocolate
1/4 C. butter
1 1/2 C. confectioners' sugar
1 egg white
1 tsp vanilla extract

Directions

1. In a small heavy pan, add the chocolate and butter on low heat and melt completely.
2. Remove from the heat and stir to combine.
3. Add the powdered sugar, egg white and vanilla and beat till smooth, adding a little water, if required.
4. Place the frosted over Chocolate Frosted Marshmallow Cookies evenly.

Spicy Mexican Vegan Fudge Truffles

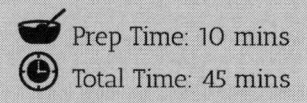

🍲 Prep Time: 10 mins
🕐 Total Time: 45 mins

Servings per Recipe: 12
Calories   258 kcal
Fat   6.2 g
Carbohydrates   53.7g
Protein   1.5 g
Cholesterol   0 mg
Sodium   32 mg

Ingredients

- 1/2 C. almond milk
- 2 tbsp margarine
- 4 C. confectioners' sugar
- 1 C. dark chocolate chips
- 1/2 C. cocoa powder
- 1/2 tsp vanilla extract
- 1/2 tsp cayenne pepper
- 1/2 tsp ground cinnamon

Directions

1. In a pan, add the milk and margarine on medium-low heat and bring to a simmer.
2. Cook for about 5 minutes.
3. In a bowl, mix together the confectioners' sugar, chocolate chips, cocoa powder, vanilla extract, cayenne pepper and ground cinnamon.
4. Place the hot milk mixture over the sugar mixture and mix till smooth.
5. Transfer the mixture into a glass baking dish evenly.
6. Refrigerate the fudge for at least 30 minutes.

AUTHENTIC
Dublin Fudge

Prep Time: 15 mins
Total Time: 30 mins

Servings per Recipe: 32
Calories   135 kcal
Fat   4.6 g
Carbohydrates   23.1g
Protein   0.3 g
Cholesterol   13 mg
Sodium   25 mg

Ingredients

1/2 C. evaporated milk
1 C. light brown sugar, packed
1 C. white sugar
3/4 C. unsalted butter, room temperature
1/4 tsp salt

1/4 C. Irish cream liqueur
1 tsp vanilla extract
2 1/4 C. confectioners' sugar, sifted

Directions

1. Grease an 8-inch square baking dish and then, line with 2 14-inch long parchment papers.
2. In a heavy pan, mix together the evaporated milk, light brown sugar, white sugar, unsalted butter and salt on medium heat and bring to a boil
3. Reduce the heat to medium-low and cook for about 20-30 minutes, stirring occasionally.
4. Remove from the heat and add the Irish cream liqueur and vanilla extract and mix till well combined.
5. Transfer the mixture into the work bowl of a large stand mixer fitted with the beaters.
6. Add the confectioners' sugar in 3 additions and blend on low speed till well combined and smooth.
7. Transfer the fudge into the prepared baking dish and refrigerate for about 3-5 hours.
8. Carefully, lift the parchment paper ends as handles to remove the fudge from the the baking dish.
9. Cut into desired sized cubes and serve.

Country Fudge Pie

🥣 Prep Time: 10 mins
🕐 Total Time: 45 mins

Servings per Recipe: 8
Calories   350 kcal
Fat   20.5 g
Carbohydrates   39.5g
Protein   3.9 g
Cholesterol   77 mg
Sodium   217 mg

Ingredients

1 recipe pastry for a 9 inch single crust pie
1 C. white sugar
1/4 C. all-purpose flour
3 tbsp unsweetened cocoa powder
1/2 C. butter
2 eggs
1 tsp vanilla extract

Directions

1. Unfold piecrust; fit into 9 inch pie pan. Prebake crust according to package
2. Directions. Remove from oven.
3. Lower the oven temperature to 325 degrees F 165 degrees C.
4. Beat together sugar, flour, cocoa powder, butter or margarine, eggs and vanilla in a medium-size bowl. Spoon into pie shell.
5. Bake for 25 to 30 minutes or until set. Allow to cool to room temperature. Serve with whipped topping or a scoop of vanilla ice cream.

SEMISWEET
Valentine's Cookies

🥣 Prep Time: 15 mins
🕒 Total Time: 30 mins

Servings per Recipe: 18
Calories	228 kcal
Fat	12.8 g
Carbohydrates	28.7g
Protein	3.7 g
Cholesterol	36 mg
Sodium	73 mg

Ingredients

7 1 oz. squares semisweet chocolate, chopped
2 1 oz. squares unsweetened chocolate, chopped
3 tbsp butter, softened
1 C. white sugar
3 eggs
1 tsp vanilla extract

3/4 C. all-purpose flour
1/2 tsp baking powder
1/4 tsp salt
1 C. semisweet chocolate chips
1/2 C. chopped walnuts

Directions

1. Set your oven to 350 degrees F before doing anything else and lightly, grease a baking sheet.
2. In the top of a double boiler, add the chopped chocolates on simmering water till melted completely, stirring occasionally.
3. Remove from hot water and keep aside to cool slightly.
4. In a bowl, mix together the flour, baking powder and salt.
5. In another bowl, add the sugar and eggs and beat till thick and creamy.
6. Add the vanilla and melted chocolate and mix well.
7. Add the flour mixture and mix till well combined.
8. Fold in the chocolate chips and walnuts.
9. With tspfuls, place the mixture onto the prepared baking sheet about 1-1/2-inch apart.
10. Cook in the oven for about 8 minutes.
11. Remove from the oven and cool on wire rack for about 3-5 minutes.
12. Invert onto racks to cool completely.

Country Fudge

Prep Time: 5 mins
Total Time: 2 hrs 25 mins

Servings per Recipe: 20
Calories   160 kcal
Fat   3.6 g
Carbohydrates   32.3g
Protein   1.1 g
Cholesterol   0 mg
Sodium   39 mg

Ingredients

3 C. white sugar, divided
1/4 C. boiling water
1 C. liquid non-dairy creamer
1/4 tsp salt
2 tsp grated orange peel

1 C. chopped almonds

Directions

1. Grease an 8x8-inch square baking dish.
2. In a heavy pan, add 1 C. of the sugar on medium heat and cook till melted completely, stirring continuously.
3. Carefully stir in the boiling water.
4. Add the remaining 2 C. of the sugar, non-dairy creamer and salt and bring to a boil, stirring continuously.
5. Now cook the mixture to 242-248 degrees F, without stirring.
6. Remove from the heat and keep aside in room temperature to cool.
7. After cooling, beat the mixture well.
8. Immediately gently, fold in the grated orange peel and almonds.
9. Transfer the mixture into the prepared pan evenly.
10. Refrigerate to chill for about 2 hours.

ZESTY
Fudge

Prep Time: 20 mins
Total Time: 2 hrs 45 mins

Servings per Recipe: 64
Calories 102 kcal
Fat 4.6 g
Carbohydrates 14.1g
Protein 1.5 g
Cholesterol 6 mg
Sodium 63 mg

Ingredients

- 1/3 C. unsalted butter, melted
- 1/4 C. sugar
- 1 1/4 14.4 oz. packages graham cracker crumbs
- 1 14 oz. can sweetened condensed milk
- 1 11 oz. package white chocolate chips such as NestleR
- 1 4 oz. bar white chocolate such as GhirardelliR
- 1/4 C. lime juice
- 1 tbsp grated lime zest

Directions

1. Set your oven to 375 degrees F before doing anything else and line an 8-inch square baking dish with greased parchment paper, leaving a 2-inch overhang.
2. In a bowl, add the butter and sugar and beat till the sugar dissolves completely.
3. Add the graham cracker crumbs and mix well.
4. Place the mixture into the bottom of the prepared baking dish and press gently to smooth the surface.
5. Cook in the oven for about 4-5 minutes.
6. Remove from the oven and keep aside to cool completely.
7. In a large pan, add the condensed milk, white chocolate chips and white chocolate on medium heat and cook, stirring continuously till the chocolate melts completely.
8. Remove the pan from heat and stir in lime juice and lime zest.
9. Place the chocolate mixture over the cooled crust.
10. With a plastic wrap, cover and refrigerate for at least 2 hours.
11. Remove the fudge by lifting the overhanging paper.
12. Cut into desired sized pieces.
13. You can preserve these fudge pieces in refrigerator by placing in an airtight container.

Fudge Kisses

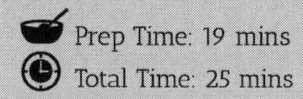

Prep Time: 19 mins
Total Time: 25 mins

Servings per Recipe: 60
Calories	94 kcal
Fat	4.5 g
Carbohydrates	13.1 g
Protein	1.5 g
Cholesterol	5 mg
Sodium	18 mg

Ingredients

- 2 C. semisweet chocolate chips
- 1/4 C. butter
- 1 14 oz. can sweetened condensed milk
- 2 C. all-purpose flour
- 1 tsp vanilla extract
- 60 milk chocolate candy kisses, unwrapped

Directions

1. Set your oven to 350 degrees F before doing anything else.
2. In a heavy pan, add the chocolate chips and butter on low heat and cook, till the mixture becomes smooth, stirring continuously.
3. Remove from the heat and stir in the condensed milk, flour and vanilla and stir till well combined.
4. Take 1 level tsp of chocolate chip dough and press around each candy kiss.
5. Arrange the bonbons onto ungreased cookie sheets in a single layer about 1-inch apart.
6. Cook in the oven for about 6 minutes.
7. Remove from the oven and keep aside to cool completely.

PARISIAN
Nutty Fudge

🥣 Prep Time: 5 mins
🕒 Total Time: 2 hrs 20 mins

Servings per Recipe: 36
Calories   156 kcal
Fat   6.6 g
Carbohydrates   23.6g
Protein   1.6 g
Cholesterol   10 mg
Sodium   49 mg

Ingredients

3/4 C. evaporated milk
2 1/2 C. white sugar
1/2 C. butter
2 C. marshmallow creme
8 oz. vanilla-flavored candy coating
1 C. chopped pistachio nuts
1 tsp vanilla extract

1 drop green food coloring

Directions

1. Grease a 13x9-inch baking dish.
2. In a pan, mix together the evaporated milk, sugar and butter on medium-high heat and bring to a boil.
3. Boil for about 4 minutes, stirring continuously.
4. Remove from the heat and add the marshmallow creme, candy coating, pistachios, vanilla and food coloring and stir till well combined.
5. Transfer the mixture into the prepared baking dish and keep aside to cool.

Oven Fudge

Prep Time: 10 mins
Total Time: 1 hr 10 mins

Servings per Recipe: 12
Calories	380 kcal
Fat	24.1 g
Carbohydrates	40.7g
Protein	4.3 g
Cholesterol	102 mg
Sodium	159 mg

Ingredients

- 2 C. white sugar
- 1/2 C. all-purpose flour
- 1/2 C. unsweetened cocoa powder
- 4 eggs, beaten
- 1 C. butter, melted
- 2 tsp vanilla extract
- 1 C. chopped pecans

Directions

1. Set your oven to 300 degrees F before doing anything else.
2. In large bowl, sift together the sugar, flour and cocoa powder.
3. Add the eggs, melted butter, vanilla and pecans and mix till well combined.
4. Transfer the mixture into a 12x8-inch baking dish.
5. Place the baking dish into a damp kitchen towel lined roasting pan and arrange the roasting pan over oven rack.
6. Add the boiling water in roasting pan, about halfway up to the sides of the baking dish.
7. Cook in the oven for about 50-60 minutes.

BERRY
Fudge

🥣 Prep Time: 5 mins
🕐 Total Time: 2 hrs 25 mins

Servings per Recipe: 20
Calories	122 kcal
Fat	0 g
Carbohydrates	31.1g
Protein	0.4 g
Cholesterol	0 mg
Sodium	6 mg

Ingredients

2 C. white sugar
1/2 C. water
1/4 tsp cream of tartar
1 C. strawberry preserves
2 egg whites, stiffly beaten

Directions

1. Grease an 8x8-inch square baking dish.
2. In a medium pan, mix together the sugar, water and cream of tartar and bring to a boil.
3. Cook till the mixture heats to 242-248 degrees F.
4. Stir in the strawberry preserves and again bring to a boil.
5. Remove from the heat.
6. In a bowl, beat the egg whites till stiff.
7. Slowly, place the strawberry mixture over the beaten egg whites, stirring continuously.
8. Then, beat the mixture till thick and fluffy.
9. Transfer the mixture into the prepared baking dish evenly and refrigerate for about 2 hours.

Buttery Peanut Fudge

Prep Time: 10 mins
Total Time: 50 mins

Servings per Recipe: 24
Calories	357 kcal
Fat	14.6 g
Carbohydrates	54.1g
Protein	5.9 g
Cholesterol	15 mg
Sodium	140 mg

Ingredients

- 4 C. white sugar
- 1 C. light brown sugar
- 1/2 C. butter
- 1 12 fluid oz. can evaporated milk
- 1 7 oz. jar marshmallow crème, optional
- 1 16 oz. jar peanut butter
- 1 tsp vanilla extract

Directions

1. Grease a 13x9-inch baking dish.
2. In a medium pan, mix together the sugar, brown sugar, butter and evaporated milk on medium heat and bring to a boil, stirring continuously.
3. Boil for about 7 minutes, stirring occasionally.
4. Remove from the heat and add the marshmallow creme and mix till melted completely.
5. Add the peanut butter and vanilla and stir till smooth.
6. Transfer the mixture into the prepared baking dish evenly.
7. Refrigerate to cool completely.
8. Cut into squares and serve.

AUGUST'S
Cheesecake

Prep Time: 30 mins
Total Time: 5 hrs

Servings per Recipe: 14
Calories   552 kcal
Fat   35.9 g
Carbohydrates   51.4g
Protein   10.6 g
Cholesterol   127 mg
Sodium   288 mg

Ingredients

1 1/2 C. vanilla wafer crumbs
1/2 C. confectioners' sugar
1/3 C. unsweetened cocoa powder
1/3 C. butter, softened
2 C. semi-sweet chocolate chips
3 8 oz. packages cream cheese, room temperature

1 14 oz. can sweetened condensed milk
4 eggs
2 tsp vanilla extract

Directions

1. Set your oven to 300 degrees F before doing anything else.
2. For the crust in a large bowl, add the crushed vanilla wafers, confectioners' sugar, cocoa and butter and with your hands mix well.
3. Place the wafers mixture into a 9-inch spring form pan evenly.
4. In the top of a double boiler, melt the chocolate chips till smooth.
5. In a large bowl, add the cream cheese and with an electric mixer, beat till fluffy.
6. Slowly, add the condensed milk, beating continuously till smooth.
7. Add the melted chocolate, eggs and vanilla and with an electric mixer, beat on low speed till well combined.
8. Place the filling over the prepared crust evenly.
9. Cook in the oven for about 55 minutes.
10. Remove from the oven and keep in the room temperature to cool.
11. Refrigerate for several hours before serving.

Fiesta Berry Brownies

Prep Time: 20 mins
Total Time: 3 hrs

Servings per Recipe: 32
Calories   135 kcal
Fat   8.4 g
Carbohydrates   14.5g
Protein   2 g
Cholesterol   33 mg
Sodium   69 mg

Ingredients

- 1 C. white sugar
- 2 eggs
- 1/2 tsp vanilla extract
- 1/2 C. butter or margarine, melted
- 1/2 C. all-purpose flour
- 1/3 C. unsweetened cocoa powder
- 1/4 tsp baking powder
- 1/4 tsp salt
- 1/2 C. miniature chocolate chips
- 1/2 C. evaporated milk
- 1 egg yolk
- 4 1 oz. squares semisweet baking chocolate, chopped
- 6 oz. cream cheese, softened
- 2 tbsp seedless raspberry jam
- 1 C. frozen whipped topping, thawed
- 2 drops red food coloring optional
- 16 chocolate curls optional

Directions

1. Set your oven to 350 degrees F before doing anything else and line an 8-inch square baking dish with a piece of foil.
2. In a large bowl, add the sugar, 2 whole eggs and vanilla and beat till well combined.
3. Add the butter and mix well.
4. In another bowl, mix together the flour, cocoa powder, baking powder and salt.
5. Add the flour mixture into the butter mixture and mix till just combined.
6. Fold in the chocolate chips.
7. Transfer the mixture into the prepared baking dish.
8. Cook in the oven for about 25-30 minutes or till a toothpick inserted in the center comes out clean.
9. Remove from the oven and keep on wire rack to cool completely.
10. In a small pan, add the evaporated milk and egg yolk and beat well on medium-low heat.

11. Cook till the mixture becomes slightly thick, stirring continuously.
12. In a bowl, add 4 oz. of the chopped semisweet chocolate.
13. Slowly, add the hot milk and stir till the chocolate melts completely.
14. Place the filling over the cooled brownies evenly and refrigerate for about 2 hours.
15. For the frosting in a large bowl, add the cream cheese and raspberry jam and beat till smooth.
16. Fold in the whipped topping and food coloring.
17. Spread the frosting over the cooled brownies evenly.
18. With a sharp knife, cut the brownies into 16 equal sized squares.
19. Now, make the triangles by cutting each square in half diagonally.

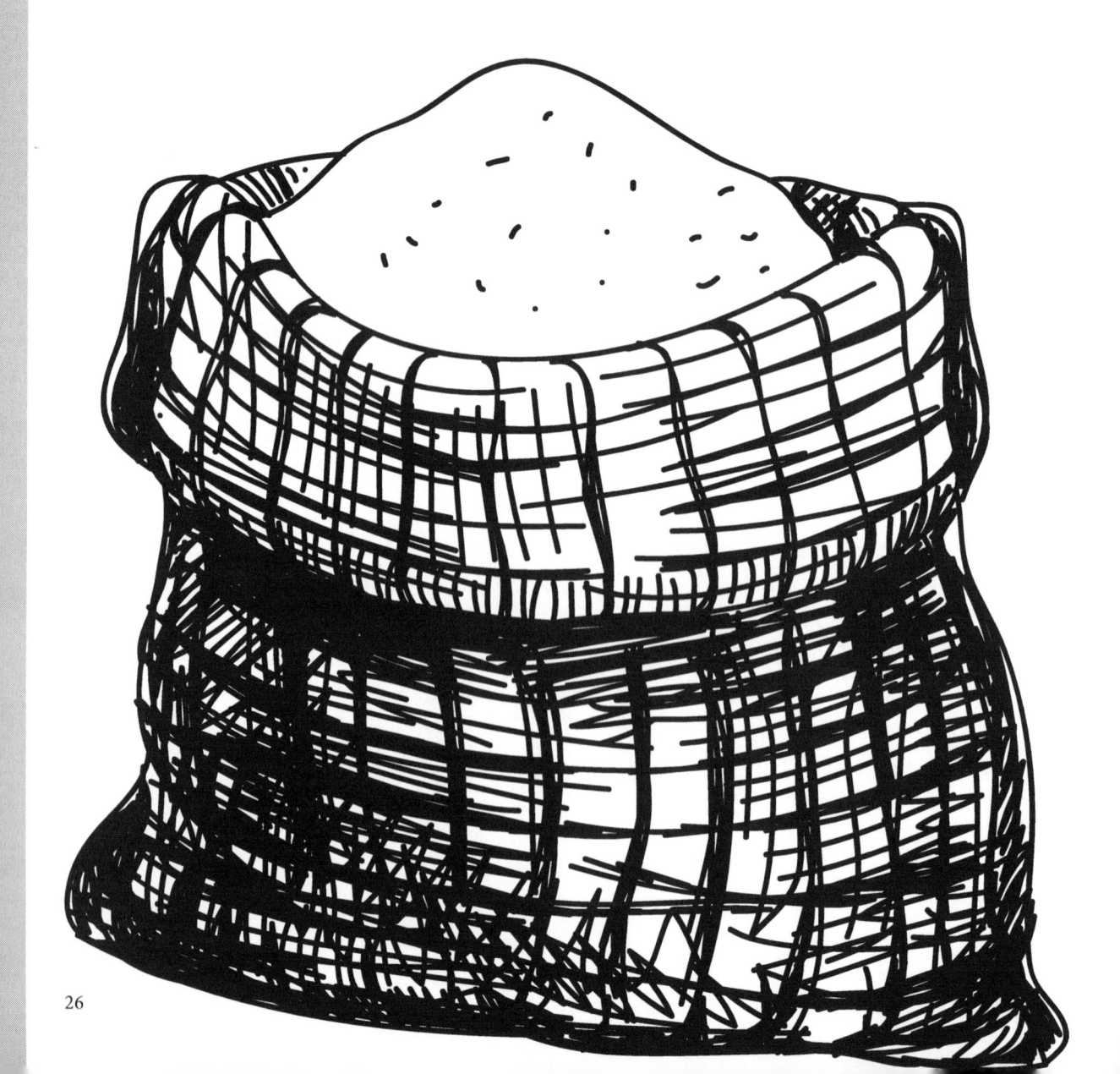

Nutty Fudge for November

Prep Time: 10 mins
Total Time: 2 hrs 15 mins

Servings per Recipe: 24
Calories   248 kcal
Fat   11.8 g
Carbohydrates   36.3g
Protein   2.6 g
Cholesterol   11 mg
Sodium   135 mg

Ingredients

- 1 7 oz. jar marshmallow crème, optional
- 1 1/2 C. white sugar
- 1 5 oz. can evaporated milk
- 1/4 C. butter
- 1/2 tsp salt
- 2 C. milk chocolate chips
- 1 C. semisweet chocolate chips
- 1 C. salted whole cashews
- 1/2 C. cherry-flavored dried cranberries
- 1 tsp vanilla extract

Directions

1. Line an 8-inch square baking dish with a piece of foil.
2. In a pan, add the marshmallow creme, sugar, evaporated milk, butter and salt and bring to a boil, stirring continuously.
3. Cook for about 5 minutes, stirring continuously.
4. Remove from the heat and add the chocolate chips, stirring continuously till melted completely.
5. Fold in the cashews, dried cranberries and vanilla extract.
6. Transfer the mixture into the prepared baking dish even and refrigerate for about 2 hours.
7. With a sharp knife, cut into 1-inch squares and serve.

FOOD CAKE
Cookies

🥣 Prep Time: 10 mins
🕙 Total Time: 20 mins

Servings per Recipe: 24
Calories	173 kcal
Fat	10.5 g
Carbohydrates	20.2g
Protein	2.1 g
Cholesterol	18 mg
Sodium	184 mg

Ingredients

- 1 18.25 oz. package devil's food cake mix
- 2 eggs
- 1/2 C. vegetable oil
- 1 C. semi-sweet chocolate chips

Directions

1. Set your oven to 350 degrees F before doing anything else and grease the cookie sheets.
2. In a bowl, add the cake mix, eggs and oil and mix till well combined.
3. Fold in the chocolate chips.
4. Make walnut sized balls from the mixture and arrange onto the prepared cookies in a single layer about 2-inch apart.
5. With your hands, press each ball slightly.
6. Cook in the oven for about 8-10 minutes.
7. Remove from the oven and keep on wire rack to cool for about 5 minutes.
8. Carefully, invert onto wire rack to cool completely.

Fudge Oat Rectangles

Prep Time: 20 mins
Total Time: 45 mins

Servings per Recipe: 30
Calories	297 kcal
Fat	13.2 g
Carbohydrates	42.4g
Protein	4.5 g
Cholesterol	35 mg
Sodium	235 mg

Ingredients

- 1 C. butter, softened
- 2 C. packed brown sugar
- 2 eggs
- 2 tsp vanilla extract
- 1/2 tsp almond extract
- 3 C. quick-cooking oats
- 2 1/2 C. all-purpose flour
- 1/2 C. sliced almonds
- 1 tsp baking soda
- 1 tsp salt

Filling:
- 2 C. semisweet chocolate chips
- 1 14 oz. can sweetened condensed milk
- 2 tbsp butter
- 1/2 tsp salt
- 2 tsp vanilla extract
- 1/2 tsp almond extract

Directions

1. Set your oven to 350 degrees F before doing anything else.
2. In a large bowl, add 1 C. of the butter and brown sugar and beat till creamy and smooth.
3. Add the eggs, 2 tsp of the vanilla extract and 1/2 tsp of the almond extract and mix well.
4. In another bowl, mix together the oats, flour, sliced almonds, baking soda and 1 tsp of the salt.
5. Add the flour mixture into the butter mixture and mix till just combined.
6. Place about 2/3 of the mixture into a 15x10-inch rimmed baking sheet evenly.
7. In a pan, add the chocolate chips, condensed milk, 2 tbsp of the butter and 1/2 tsp of the salt on medium heat and cook for about 5 minutes, stirring occasionally.
8. Remove from the heat and stir in the remaining 2 tsp of the vanilla extract and 1/2 tsp of the almond extract.
9. Place the chocolate mixture over the oat mixture evenly and top with the remaining 1/3 of the oat mixture.
10. Cook in the oven for about 20-25 minutes.

CANDY
Gravy

Prep Time: 5 mins
Total Time: 15 mins

Servings per Recipe: 16
Calories	136 kcal
Fat	9.4 g
Carbohydrates	14.8g
Protein	1.3 g
Cholesterol	8 mg
Sodium	46 mg

Ingredients

- 30 large marshmallows, optional
- 2/3 C. milk
- 1/4 C. butter
- 1/8 tsp salt
- 1 12 oz. package semisweet chocolate chips
- 1 1/2 tsp vanilla extract

Directions

1. In a pan, add the marshmallows, milk, butter and salt on low heat and cook for about 5 minutes, stirring occasionally.
2. Add the chocolate chips and vanilla extract and cook for about 5 minutes, stirring continuously.
3. Serve this sauce warm.

Caribbean Creamy Fudge

Prep Time: 3 mins
Total Time: 11 mins

Servings per Recipe: 12
Calories   489.7
Fat   21.8g
Cholesterol   30.3mg
Sodium   162.8mg
Carbohydrates   72.7g
Protein   3.2g

Ingredients

- 1 12 oz. bags white chocolate chips
- 1 6 oz. bags flaked coconut
- 1/2 C. butter
- 2 C. sugar
- 2/3 C. evaporated milk
- 1 tsp coconut flavoring
- 1 7 oz. jars marshmallow crème, optional

Directions

1. In a large pan, add the butter, sugar and milk on medium heat and bring to boil, stirring continuously.
2. Boil for about 5 minutes, stirring continuously.
3. Remove from the heat and stir in the marshmallow crème and white chocolate chips till the chips are melted.
4. Stir in the coconut and coconut flavoring.
5. Transfer the mixture into medium greased baking dish evenly.
6. Keep in the room temperature to cool completely.
7. Now, refrigerate till firm.

3-INGREDIENT Peanut Butter Candy

Prep Time: 5 mins
Total Time: 10 mins

Servings per Recipe: 1
Calories   93.2
Fat   7.7g
Cholesterol   1.3mg
Sodium   28.8mg
Carbohydrates   6.5g
Protein   2.3g

Ingredients

1 lb white chocolate
12 oz. peanut butter, chunky style
1 lb semisweet chocolate, melted

Directions

1. In the top of a double boiler, mix together the white chocolate and peanut butter and bring the water to a boil.
2. Reduce the heat to low and melt the mixture completely, stirring continuously.
3. Place the mixture onto a waxed paper lined 15x10x1-inch jellyroll pan evenly.
4. Spread the melted semisweet chocolate over the peanut butter mixture and with a knife, swirl through.
5. Refrigerate till firm.
6. Cut into 1 1/2x1-inch sized pieces and serve.
7. You can preserve these squares in in refrigerator by placing in an airtight container.

Lover's Fudge Sauce

Prep Time: 4 hrs
Total Time: 4 hrs 15 mins

Servings per Recipe: 1
Calories   3170.1
Fat   136.9g
Cholesterol   111.5mg
Sodium   1049.2mg
Carbohydrates   450.5g
Protein   31.1g

Ingredients

- 1 1/3 C. sugar
- 7 oz. marshmallow creme
- 2/3 C. evaporated milk
- 1/4 C. butter
- 1/4 C. Kahlua, optional
- 1/4 tsp salt
- 2 C. semisweet chocolate pieces
- 1 C. milk chocolate pieces
- 2/3 C. chopped nuts
- 1 tsp vanilla

Directions

1. Line an 8-inch square baking dish with a piece of foil.
2. In 2-quart pan, mix together the sugar, marshmallow crème, milk, butter, Kahlua and salt and bring to a boil, stirring continuously.
3. Boil for about 5 minutes, stirring continuously.
4. Remove from the heat and stir in the both chocolates till melted.
5. Stir in the nuts and vanilla.
6. Place the mixture into the prepared baking dish evenly and refrigerate till firm.
7. Cut into equal sized squares and serve.

WALDORF
Fudge

Prep Time: 2 mins
Total Time: 7 mins

Servings per Recipe: 1
Calories 210.7
Fat 10.1g
Cholesterol 8.9mg
Sodium 54.5mg
Carbohydrates 31.1g
Protein 3.1g

Ingredients

2 1/2 C. semi-sweet chocolate chips
1 14 oz. cans condensed milk
1/8 tsp salt

Directions

1. In a pan, melt the the semi-sweet chocolate chips.
2. Remove from the heat and stir in the condensed milk and salt till well combined.
3. Place the mixture into a buttered 9-inch baking dish evenly.
4. Refrigerate till set.

Gloria's Fudge Dip

Prep Time: 10 mins
Total Time: 40 mins

Servings per Recipe: 24
Calories 94.5
Fat 2.5g
Cholesterol 7.5mg
Sodium 38.2mg
Carbohydrates 17.5g
Protein 0.6g

Ingredients

2 C. sugar
2/3 C. evaporated milk
1/3 C. milk
1/8 tsp salt
1/4 C. butter

1 tbsp vanilla
walnut pieces optional

Directions

1. Grease the sides of a 2 quart heavy pan.
2. In the greased pan, mix together the sugar, both milk and salt on medium heat and bring to a boil, stirring continuously.
3. Reduce the heat to medium-low and cook till the temperature reaches to 238 degrees F.
4. Remove from the heat and add the butter and vanilla.
5. Keep aside to cool till the temperature reaches to 110 degrees F.
6. With a wooden spoon, beat till the fudge becomes thick.
7. Place the mixture into a buttered 8-inch baking dish evenly.
8. Refrigerate to chill before serving.

PECAN
Snack

🥣 Prep Time: 15 mins
🕐 Total Time: 20 mins

Servings per Recipe: 1
Calories	60.9
Fat	3.4g
Cholesterol	6.7mg
Sodium	19.7mg
Carbohydrates	7.7g
Protein	0.2g

Ingredients

1/2 C. butter
1/2 C. heavy cream
1/2 C. granulated sugar
1/2 C. packed light brown sugar
1/8 tsp salt

1 C. pecan halves, toasted
1 tsp vanilla extract
2 C. confectioners' sugar

Directions

1. Grease an 8-inch square baking dish with the nonstick cooking spray.
2. In a large pan, add the butter, heavy cream, granulated sugar, brown sugar and salt on medium heat and bring to a boil, stirring occasionally.
3. Boil for about 5 minutes, stirring.
4. Remove from the heat and stir in the pecans and vanilla.
5. Add the confections' sugar and stir till smooth.
6. Place the mixture into the prepared baking dish.
7. Keep in the room temperature to cool.
8. Cut into 1-inch sized squares and serve.
9. You can preserve these squares in refrigerator by placing in an airtight container.

Swiss Candy Fudge

Prep Time: 10 mins
Total Time: 3 hrs 20 mins

Servings per Recipe: 25
Calories   58.1
Fat   4.2g
Cholesterol   11.9mg
Sodium   34.1mg
Carbohydrates   4.7g
Protein   0.5g

Ingredients

1/2 C. sugar
1/2 C. butter
3/4 C. evaporated milk

1 400 g Toblerone chocolate bars, broken into pieces

Directions

1. Line an 8-inch square baking dish with a parchment paper, with ends of paper extending over sides of the dish.
2. In large, heavy pan, add the sugar, butter and evaporated milk on medium heat and bring to a full rolling boil, stirring continuously.
3. Boil for about 5 minutes, stirring continuously.
4. Remove from the heat and stir in the chocolate till melted completely.
5. Place the mixture into the prepared baking dish evenly and refrigerate for about 3 hours.
6. With paper handles, remove the fudge from the baking dish.
7. Cut into 25 equal sized squares.
8. You can preserve these squares in refrigerator by placing in an airtight container.

FUDGE
on a Stick

Prep Time: 10 mins
Total Time: 10 mins

Servings per Recipe: 1
Calories	165.3
Fat	5.8g
Cholesterol	19.3mg
Sodium	67.1mg
Carbohydrates	24.9g
Protein	3.7g

Ingredients

1/2 C. sugar
2 tbsp cornstarch
2 tbsp Hersheys cocoa powder
2 1/2 C. milk
1 tsp vanilla

1 tbsp butter

Directions

1. In a small pan, mix together the sugar, cornstarch, cocoa and milk on medium and cook till thick, stirring continuously.
2. Remove from the heat and stir in the vanilla and butter till well combined.
3. Divide the mixture into the ice-pop molds evenly.
4. Insert the ice-pop sticks and freeze till firm.

Fudge in Moscow

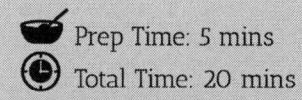

Prep Time: 5 mins
Total Time: 20 mins

Servings per Recipe: 24
Calories   160.1
Fat   4.9 g
Cholesterol   14.0 mg
Sodium   60.4 mg
Carbohydrates   29.4 g
Protein   0.7 g

Ingredients

- 3 C. sugar
- 1/2 C. milk
- 1/2 C. sweetened condensed milk
- 125 g butter
- 1/8 tsp salt
- 1 tbsp golden syrup

Directions

1. In a pan, add the sugar and milk and cook till the sugar is dissolved, stirring continuously.
2. Add the condensed milk, butter, salt and golden syrup and cook till the butter is melted, stirring continuously.
3. Bring to a boil and the boil till the temperature reaches to 234 degrees F, stirring occasionally.
4. Remove from the heat and keep aside to cool slightly.
5. Now, beat the mixture till thick.
6. Transfer the mixture into a greased baking dish and refrigerate to set.
7. Cut into equal sized squares and serve.

NOVEMBER ONLY
Fudge

Prep Time: 30 mins
Total Time: 1 hr

Servings per Recipe: 1
Calories   1432.8
Fat   67.9g1
Cholesterol   97.2mg
Sodium   446.2mg
Carbohydrates   205.6g
Protein   9.2g

Ingredients

2 C. sugar
1 C. firmly packed brown sugar
3/4 C. butter
2/3 C. evaporated milk
1/2 C. canned pumpkin
1 1/2-2 tsp pumpkin pie spice
1 12 oz. packages white chocolate chips

1 7 oz. jars marshmallow crème, optional
1 C. chopped pecans
1 1/2 tsp vanilla extract

Directions

1. In a heavy pan, mix together the sugar, brown sugar, butter, evaporated milk, pumpkin and pumpkin pie spice on medium heat and cook till sugar is dissolved, stirring occasionally.
2. Bring to a boil, stirring continuously.
3. Boiling till the temperature reaches to 234-243 degrees F.
4. Remove from the heat and stir in the chocolate chips till melted completely.
5. Add the remaining ingredients and mix well.
6. Place the mixture into a buttered 13x9-inch baking dish and keep in room temperature to cool.
7. Cut into equal sized squares.
8. You can preserve these squares in refrigerator by placing in an airtight container.

Microwave Chocolate Butter

Prep Time: 10 mins
Total Time: 22 mins

Servings per Recipe: 24
Calories   284.3
Fat   13.6g
Cholesterol   16.9mg
Sodium   65.8mg
Carbohydrates   42.2g
Protein   1.8g

Ingredients

3/4 C. butter
3 C. sugar
1 5 oz. cans evaporated milk
1 12 oz. packages semi-sweet chocolate chips
1 7 oz. jars marshmallow crème, optional
1 tsp vanilla

1 C. chopped walnuts

Directions

1. In a microwave safe bowl, add the butter and microwave on High for about 1 minute.
2. Stir in the sugar and milk and microwave on High for about 5 minutes, stirring after every 3 minutes.
3. Stir the mixture and well and microwave on High for about 5 1/2 minutes, stirring after every 3 minutes.
4. Remove from the microwave and keep aside for about 2 minutes.
5. Stir in the chocolate chips till melted.
6. Add the marshmallow crème and vanilla and mix well.
7. Stir in the walnuts.
8. Place the mixture into a generously buttered 13x9-inch baking dish.
9. Keep aside in the room temperature to cool.
10. Cut into equal sized squares.

CREAM CHEESE
Fudge

🥣 Prep Time: 30 mins
🕐 Total Time: 3o mins

Servings per Recipe: 1
Calories 2476.1
Fat 122.9g1
Cholesterol 129.4mg
Sodium 431.4mg
Carbohydrates 338.4g
Protein 20.0g

Ingredients

2 3 oz. packages cream cheese, softened
1 16 oz. packages powdered sugar, sifted
1 1/2 tsp vanilla extract
1 12 oz. white chocolate baking bar, melted

1 C. chopped pecans, toasted

Directions

1. In a bowl, add the cream cheese and with an electric mixer, beat on medium speed till fluffy.
2. Slowly, add the sugar and beat well.
3. Add the vanilla and melted white chocolate and stir till well combined.
4. Fold in the chopped pecans.
5. Place the mixture into a buttered 8-inch square baking dish evenly.
6. Refrigerate, covered till set.

Morning Coffee Fudge

Prep Time: 4 hrs
Total Time: 4 hrs 15 mins

Servings per Recipe: 1
Calories   1354.9
Fat   81.2g1
Cholesterol   72.8mg
Sodium   279.9mg
Carbohydrates   167.5g
Protein   13.1g

Ingredients

- 1 7 oz. jars marshmallow cream, optional
- 1/2 C. sugar
- 2/3 C. whipping cream
- 1/4 C. whipped margarine
- 1 tsp instant coffee
- 1/4 tsp ground cinnamon
- 1/4 tsp salt
- 1 12 oz. bags semi-sweet chocolate chips
- 1 C. toasted chopped hazelnuts

Directions

1. Line an 8-inch square baking dish with a piece of foil.
2. In a 2 qt pan, mix together the marshmallow cream, sugar, cream, margarine, coffee powder, cinnamon and salt on medium heat and bring to a boil, stirring continuously.
3. Boil for about 5 minutes, stirring continuously.
4. Remove from the heat and stir in the chocolate chips till smooth.
5. Stir in the hazelnuts.
6. Place the mixture into the prepared baking dish evenly.
7. Refrigerate, covered for about overnight.
8. By lifting the foil, remove the fudge onto cutting board.
9. Cut into 36 equal sized squares and serve.

FUDGE
Mud Drink

Prep Time: 5 mins
Total Time: 10 mins

Servings per Recipe: 6
Calories 185.7
Fat 5.1g
Cholesterol 15.9mg
Sodium 57.3mg
Carbohydrates 34.4g
Protein 5.1g

Ingredients

3/4 C. granulated sugar
1/2 C. baking cocoa
2 2/3 C. milk 1% fat
2 tbsp milk 1% fat

Directions

1. In a pan, mix together the sugar and cocoa.
2. Slowly, add 2 2/3 C. of the milk, stirring continuously.
3. Cook on low heat till the sugar is dissolved, stirring continuously.
4. Divide the mixture into several ice cube trays.
5. Freeze, covered for overnight.
6. Remove the frozen mixture from the ice trays and break into the chunks.
7. In a blender, add the broken chunks and 2 tbsp of the milk and pulse till smooth and slushy.

Fudge
Lunch Box Crisps

Prep Time: 30 mins
Total Time: 40 mins

Servings per Recipe: 1
Calories   209.5
Fat   9.1g
Cholesterol   21.3mg
Sodium   155.7mg
Carbohydrates   31.6g
Protein   1.0g

Ingredients

1 11 1/2 oz. packages milk chocolate chips
1/2 C. butter
1/2 C. light corn syrup
2 tsp vanilla
1 C. powdered sugar
4 C. Rice Krispies

Directions

1. In a pan, mix together the milk chocolate chips, butter and corn syrup on low heat and cook till the mixture becomes smooth.
2. Remove from the heat and stir in the vanilla and sugar.
3. Add the Rice Krispies and gently, mix till well combined.
4. Place the mixture into a buttered 13x9-inch baking dish.
5. Refrigerate to chill till firm.
6. Cut into desired sized squares.
7. You can preserve these squares in refrigerator by placing in an airtight container.

FUDGE
Milk

🥣 Prep Time: 15 mins
🕐 Total Time: 1 hr 15 mins

Servings per Recipe: 12
Calories 210.4
Fat 7.8g
Cholesterol 21.1mg
Sodium 194.2mg
Carbohydrates 35.5g
Protein 0.7g

Ingredients

2 C. granulated sugar
1 C. buttermilk
1/2 C. butter
1 tbsp corn syrup

1 tsp baking soda
1 tsp vanilla extract
1/2 C. chopped nuts

Directions

1. Grease the sides of a large heavy pan.
2. In the greased pan. Add the granulated sugar, buttermilk, butter, corn syrup and baking soda on medium-low heat and cook till the sugar dissolves, stirring continuously.
3. Dip a pastry brush in hot water and wash down any sugar crystals on side of the pan.
4. Increase the heat to medium and bring to a boil without stirring.
5. Cook till the temperature of the mixture reaches to 234-40 degrees.
6. Remove from the heat and stir in the vanilla.
7. Keep aside till the temperature of the mixture reaches to 200 degrees.
8. With an electric mixer, beat the fudge on medium speed till the mixture becomes thick.
9. Stir in the nuts.
10. Transfer the mixture into a greased 8-inch square baking dish and cool completely.
11. Cut into 1-inch sized squares and serve.
12. You can preserve these squares in refrigerator by placing in an airtight container.

Christmas Fudge Drink

Prep Time: 2 mins
Total Time: 10 mins

Servings per Recipe: 1
Calories   4032.8
Fat   92.0g1
Cholesterol   210.8mg
Sodium   512.4mg
Carbohydrates   810.8g
Protein   15.1g

Ingredients

- 1 C. non-alcoholic eggnog
- 3 C. sugar
- 1 1/2 C. miniature marshmallows, optional
- 1/2 tsp cinnamon
- 1/2 tsp nutmeg
- 1/8 C. butter, chilled
- 6 oz. butterscotch chips
- 1 C. chopped almonds optional
- butter-flavored cooking spray

Directions

1. Line a 9 inch square baking dish with a piece of foil.
2. Grease the sides of a large pan with butter flavored nonstick cooking spray.
3. In the greased pan, add the egg nog and sugar on medium heat and bring to a boil, stirring continuously.
4. Boil for about 2 minutes exactly and immediately, reduce the heat to low.
5. Keep on low heat, stirring occasionally.
6. Fold in marshmallows, cinnamon and nutmeg and stir till the marshmallows are dissolved completely.
7. Again bring to a rolling boil and then boil for about 6 minutes, stirring continuously.
8. Remove from the heat and add butter, chocolate chips and almonds and stir till well combined.
9. Transfer the mixture into the prepared baking dish and sprinkle with the nutmeg.
10. Keep aside in the room temperature to cool.
11. Remove from the baking dish and cut into 1-inch squares.
12. You can preserve these squares in an airtight container.

MARIA'S
Cinnamon Fudge

🥣 Prep Time: 10 mins
🕐 Total Time: 10 mins

Servings per Recipe: 20
Calories	125.5
Fat	3.3g
Cholesterol	8.7mg
Sodium	74.4mg
Carbohydrates	23.5g
Protein	1.0g

Ingredients

2 C. sugar
1 C. evaporated milk
3 tbsp unsalted butter
1/4 tsp cinnamon
1/2 tsp salt

1/2 C. miniature marshmallow
1 1/2 C. milk chocolate chips
1 tsp vanilla

Directions

1. Set your electric skillet to 280 degrees F.
2. Immediately, add the sugar, evaporated milk, butter, cinnamon and salt and bring to a boil, stirring continuously.
3. Boil for about minutes, stirring continuously.
4. Unplug the skillet and stir in the marshmallows, chocolate chips and vanilla till well combined.
5. Transfer the mixture into a greased pie dish evenly.
6. Refrigerate to cool completely.
7. Cut into desired sized pieces and serve.

5-Ingredient Pralines

Prep Time: 10 mins
Total Time: 40 mins

Servings per Recipe: 10
Calories   316.5
Fat   18.9g
Cholesterol   22.0mg
Sodium   68.7mg
Carbohydrates   35.7g
Protein   3.8g

Ingredients

12 oz. evaporated milk
1 1/2 C. sugar
1/4 C. butter
1 tsp vanilla extract
1 1/2 C. pecans

Directions

1. In a pan, add the milk and sugar and bring to a boil.
2. Add the butter and vanilla and cook till the temperature reaches to 235 degrees F.
3. Stir in 1-1/2 C. of the pecans and cook till the temperature reaches to 240 degrees F.
4. Remove from the heat and beat till thick.
5. With the spoonfuls, place the mixture over a greased baking sheet and keep aside to cool completely.

CANADIAN STYLE
Fudge

🥣 Prep Time: 5 mins
🕐 Total Time: 20 mins

Servings per Recipe: 4
Calories   916.9
Fat   41.9g
Cholesterol   104.2mg
Sodium   356.6mg
Carbohydrates   131.2g
Protein   9.6g

Ingredients

125 g butter
2 tbsp golden syrup
400 g sweetened condensed milk
1 C. brown sugar

100 g white chocolate chips

Directions

1. In a pan, melt the butter.
2. Add the golden syrup, sweetened condensed milk and brown sugar on medium-low heat and bring to a boil.
3. Reduce the heat to low and simmer for about 10 minutes, stirring continuously.
4. Remove from the heat and immediately stir in the white chocolate chips till melted and smooth.
5. Transfer the mixture into a foil lined 7x25-inch bar pan and refrigerate till sets completely.
6. Cut into desired sized squares and serve.

4-Ingredient Fudge Shells

Prep Time: 2 mins
Total Time: 13 mins

Servings per Recipe: 1
Calories 83.1
Fat 4.1g
Cholesterol 4.0mg
Sodium 46.3mg
Carbohydrates 10.3g
Protein 1.3g

Ingredients

- nonstick cooking spray
- 9 oz. packages refrigerated peanut butter cookie dough
- 1/2 C. semisweet chocolate piece
- 1/4 C. sweetened condensed milk

Directions

1. Set your oven to 350 degrees F before doing anything else and grease 24 1 3/4-inch muffin cups with the cooking spray.
2. For tart shells, cut cookie dough into 6 equal sized pieces and then cut each piece into 4 equal sized slices.
3. Arrange 1 dough slice into each prepared muffin cup.
4. Cook in the oven for about 9 minutes.
5. Remove the tart shells from the oven.
6. With the back of a round 1/2 tsp measuring spoon, gently press a shallow indentation in each tart shell.
7. Cook in the oven for about 2 minutes ore.
8. Remove the tart shells from the oven and keep onto a wire rack for about 15 minutes.
9. Carefully remove the tart shells from the muffin cups and keep onto wire rack to cool completely.
10. For filling in a small pan, mix together the chocolate pieces and sweetened condensed milk on medium heat and cook till the chocolate is melted, stirring continuously.
11. With a teaspoon, place a little chocolate mixture into each cooled tart shell and keep aside till the filling is set.

FUDGE
Festivals

Prep Time: 25 mins
Total Time: 25 mins

Servings per Recipe: 1
Calories	4060.4
Fat	190.3g2
Cholesterol	191.3mg
Sodium	1123.7mg
Carbohydrates	606.9g
Protein	30.9g

Ingredients

1 6 oz. packages semi-sweet chocolate chips
2 3 oz. packages cream cheese, at room temperature
2 tbsp milk
4 C. sifted confectioners' sugar 10X

1 tsp vanilla extract
1/4 tsp salt
1 C. coarsely chopped pecans

Directions

1. Grease a 9x9x2-inch baking dish.
2. Place the chocolate chips in a double boiler on hot water and melt completely.
3. In a bowl, add the cream cheese and milk and with an electric mixer, beat on high speed till smooth.
4. Slowly, add the powdered sugar, about 1/2 C. at a time and beat on low speed till creamy.
5. Add the melted chocolate chips, vanilla and salt and beat till smooth.
6. Fold in the pecans.
7. Place the mixture into the prepared baking dish evenly.
8. With a plastic wrap, cover the baking dish and refrigerate to chill for overnight. o
9. Cut into 1 1/4-inch sized squares and serve.

Fudge Spheres

Prep Time: 15 mins
Total Time: 1 hr 15 mins

Servings per Recipe: 24
Calories   165.3
Fat   6.7g
Cholesterol   0.0mg
Sodium   177.0mg
Carbohydrates   26.7g
Protein   1.8g

Ingredients

1 18 oz. packages Duncan Hines Moist Deluxe Butter Recipe Fudge Cake Mix
1 C. pecans, finely chopped
2 C. confectioners' sugar, sifted
1/4 C. unsweetened cocoa
pecans, finely chopped

Directions

1. Set your oven to 375 degrees F before doing anything else and grease and flour a 13x9-inch baking dish.
2. Cook the cake in the oven according to package's instructions.
3. Remove from the oven and crumble the cake into large bowl.
4. With a fork, stir till the crumbs are uniform in size.
5. Add 1 C. of the pecans, confectioners' sugar and cocoa and stir till well combined.
6. With heaping tbsps, make the balls from the mixture.
7. In a shallow dish, place desired amount of the chopped pecans.
8. Coat the balls in the pecans evenly.

PURPLE
Flower Fudge

Prep Time: 10 mins
Total Time: 15 mins

Servings per Recipe: 27
Calories 138.9
Fat 7.6g
Cholesterol 8.3mg
Sodium 20.6mg
Carbohydrates 18.6g
Protein 1.8g

Ingredients

16 oz. chocolate chips
14 oz. sweetened condensed milk
1 tbsp dried lavender flowers
3 tbsp unsalted butter

Garnish
fresh lavender

Directions

1. In a clean coffee grinder, grind the chocolate chips finely.
2. In a double boiler, melt the chocolate chips, condensed milk and lavender flowers completely.
3. Add the butter and melt till smooth, stirring continuously.
4. Transfer the mixture into a wax paper lined 9x9-inch baking dish evenly.
5. With a plastic wrap, cover the baking dish and refrigerate to chill for overnight.
6. Cut into 1-inch squares and wrap in wax paper twists.
7. Decorate with fresh lavender before serving.

Fudge Tarts

Prep Time: 20 mins
Total Time: 45 mins

Servings per Recipe: 1
Calories 446.6
Fat 20.7g
Cholesterol 65.3mg
Sodium 243.3mg
Carbohydrates 63.2g
Protein 5.7g

Ingredients

- 1 C. butter, softened
- 1 C. sugar
- 2/3 C. packed light brown sugar
- 2 large eggs
- 2 tsp vanilla extract
- 2 1/2 C. flour
- 1 tsp baking soda
- 1/4 tsp salt
- 2 C. semi-sweet chocolate chips, melted
- 1 14 oz. cans sweetened condensed milk

Directions

1. Set your oven to 375 degrees F before doing anything else and grease and flour a 13x9-inch baking dish.
2. In a large bowl, add the butter and both sugars and beat till light and fluffy.
3. Add the eggs and beat well.
4. Add the vanilla and beat till smooth.
5. In another bowl, mix together the flour, baking powder and salt.
6. Add the flour mixture into the egg mixture and mix till just combined.
7. Place 1/2 of the flour mixture in the prepared baking dish evenly.
8. In a bowl, add the melted chocolate and condensed milk and mix till a fudge-like mixture forms.
9. Place the melted chocolate mixture over the flour mixture evenly and top with the remaining flour mixture.
10. Cook in the oven for about 25 minutes.
11. Remove from the oven and keep on a wire rack to cool.
12. Cut into bars and serve.

YELLOW
Parfait

Prep Time: 5 mins
Total Time: 5 mins

Servings per Recipe: 1
Calories	155.4
Cholesterol	3.6mg
Sodium	142.0mg
Carbohydrates	27.5g
Protein	11.1g

Ingredients

3/4 C. nonfat plain yogurt
1/2 C. instant chocolate fudge flavor pudding and pie filling
1/2 C. cereal

1/2 ripe banana, sliced

Directions

1. Add your pudding to a parfait glass then add the yogurt, and banana pieces.
2. Top everything with the cereal.
3. Enjoy.

ENJOY THE RECIPES?
KEEP ON COOKING WITH 6 MORE FREE COOKBOOKS!

Visit our website and simply enter your email address to join the club and receive your 6 cookbooks.

http://booksumo.com/magnet

https://www.instagram.com/booksumopress/

https://www.facebook.com/booksumo/

Printed in Poland
by Amazon Fulfillment
Poland Sp. z o.o., Wrocław